Civil War Medicine

Untold History of the Civil War

African Americans in the Civil War

Civil War Forts

The Civil War in the West

Civil War Medicine

Ironclads and Blockades in the Civil War

Prison Camps in the Civil War

Rangers, Jayhawkers, and Bushwhackers
in the Civil War

Secret Weapons in the Civil War

The Soldier's Life in the Civil War

Spies in the Civil War

The Underground Railroad and the Civil War

Women in the Civil War

CHELSEA HOUSE PUBLISHERS

Untold History of the Civil War

Civil War Medicine

Douglas J. Savage

CHELSEA HOUSE PUBLISHERS
Philadelphia

Produced by Combined Publishing
P.O. Box 307, Conshohocken, Pennsylvania 19428
1-800-418-6065
E-mail: combined@combinedpublishing.com
web: www.combinedpublishing.com

CHELSEA HOUSE PUBLISHERS

Editor in Chief: Stephen Reginald
Managing Editor: James D. Gallagher
Production Manager: Pamela Loos
Art Director: Sara Davis
Director of Photography: Judy L. Hasday
Senior Production Editor: LeeAnne Gelletly
Assistant Editor: Anne Hill

Front Cover Illustration: "Island of Mercy" by Keith Rocco. Courtesy of Tradition
Studios. Copyright © Keith Rocco.

The Chelsea House World Wide Website address is
http://www.chelseahouse.com

3 5 7 9 8 6 4 2

Library of Congress Cataloging-in-Publication Data applied for:
ISBN 0-7910-5709-7

Contents

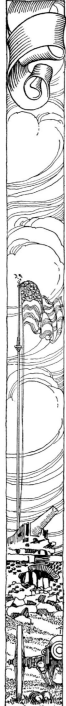

	MAPS	6-7
	CIVIL WAR CHRONOLOGY	8
I	BUILDING THE CONFEDERATE MEDICAL DEPARTMENT	11
II	EXPANDING THE FEDERAL MEDICAL DEPARTMENT	27
III	THE BATTLE AGAINST DISEASE	45
IV	THE PERILS OF DIRTY KNIVES AND BONE SAWS	53
	GLOSSARY	61
	FURTHER READING	62
	WEBSITES ABOUT MEDICINE IN THE CIVIL WAR	62
	INDEX	63

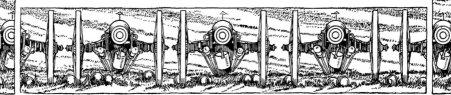

CIVIL WAR
Strategic Theater
1863

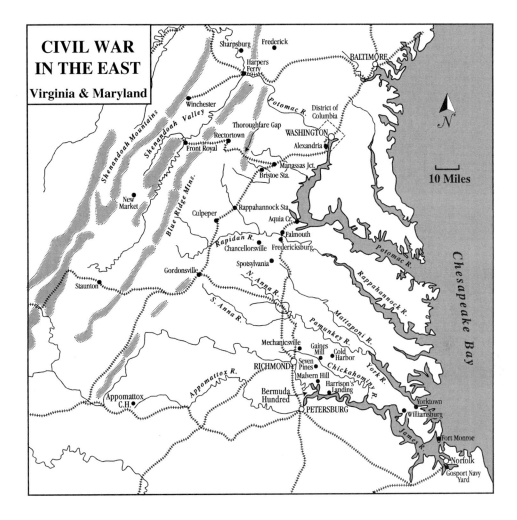

CIVIL WAR IN THE EAST

Virginia & Maryland

Sharpsburg
Frederick
BALTIMORE
Harpers Ferry
Potomac R.
Winchester
District of Columbia
Thoroughfare Gap
WASHINGTON
Rectortown
Alexandria
Front Royal
Manassas Jct.
Bristoe Sta.
New Market
Culpeper
Rappahannock Sta
Aquia Cr.
Falmouth
Rapidan R.
Chancellorsville
Fredericksburg
Spotsylvania
Gordonsville
N. Anna R.
Staunton
S. Anna R.
Potomac R.
Rappahannock R.
Mattaponi R.
Pamunkey R.
Mechanicsville
Gaines Mill
Cold Harbor
Seven Pines
York R.
RICHMOND
Chickahominy R.
Malvern Hill
Harrison's Landing
Appomattox R.
Bermuda Hundred
Appomattox C.H.
Yorktown
PETERSBURG
Williamsburg
James R.
Fort Monroe
Norfolk
Gosport Navy Yard

Shenandoah Mountains
Shenandoah Valley
Blue Ridge Mtns.

Chesapeake Bay

N

10 Miles

7

Civil War Chronology

1860
November 6 Abraham Lincoln is elected president of the United States.
December 20 South Carolina becomes the first state to secede from the Union.

1861
January-April Mississippi, Florida, Alabama, Georgia, Louisiana, and Texas also secede from the Union.
April 1 Bombardment of Fort Sumter begins the Civil War.
April-May Lincoln calls for volunteers to fight the Southern rebellion, causing a second wave of secession with Virginia, Arkansas, Tennessee, and North Carolina all leaving the Union.
May Union naval forces begin blockading the Confederate coast and reoccupying some Southern ports and offshore islands.
July 21 Union forces are defeated at the First Battle of Bull Run and withdraw to Washington.

1862
February Previously unknown Union general Ulysses S. Grant captures Confederate garrisons in Tennessee at Fort Henry (February 6) and Fort Donelson (February 16).
March 7-8 Confederates and their Cherokee allies are defeated at Pea Ridge, Arkansas.
March 8-9 Naval battle at Hampton Roads, Virginia, involving the USS *Monitor* and the CSS *Virginia* (formerly the USS *Merrimac*) begins the era of the armored fighting ship.
April-July The Union army marches on Richmond after an amphibious landing. Confederate forces block Northern advance in a series of battles. Robert E. Lee is placed in command of the main Confederate army in Virginia.
April 6-7 Grant defeats the Southern army at Shiloh Church, Tennessee, after a costly two-day battle.
April 27 New Orleans is captured by Union naval forces under Admiral David Farragut.
May 31 The battle of Seven Pines (also called Fair Oaks) is fought and the Union lines are held.
August 29-30 Lee wins substantial victory over the Army of the Potomac at the Second Battle of Bull Run near Manassas, Virginia.
September 17 Union General George B. McClellan repulses Lee's first invasion of the North at Antietam Creek near Sharpsburg, Maryland, in the bloodiest single day of the war.
November 13 Grant begins operations against the key Confederate fortress at Vicksburg, Mississippi.
December 13 Union forces suffer heavy losses storming Confederate positions at Fredericksburg, Virginia.

1863
January 1 President Lincoln issues the Emancipation Proclamation, freeing the slaves in the Southern states.

May 1-6	Lee wins an impressive victory at Chancellorsville, but key Southern commander Thomas J. "Stonewall" Jackson dies of wounds, an irreplaceable loss for the Army of Northern Virginia.
June	The city of Vicksburg and the town of Port Hudson are held under siege by the Union army. They surrender on July 4.
July 1-3	Lee's second invasion of the North is decisively defeated at Gettysburg, Pennsylvania.
July 16	Union forces led by the black 54th Massachusetts Infantry attempt to regain control of Fort Sumter by attacking the Fort Wagner outpost.
September 19-20	Confederate victory at Chickamauga, Georgia, gives some hope to the South after disasters at Gettysburg and Vicksburg.

1864

February 17	A new Confederate submarine, the *Hunley,* attacks and sinks the USS *Housatonic* in the waters off Charleston.
March 9	General Grant is made supreme Union commander. He decides to campaign in the East with the Army of the Potomac while General William T. Sherman carries out a destructive march across the South from the Mississippi to the Atlantic coast.
May-June	In a series of costly battles (Wilderness, Spotsylvania, and Cold Harbor), Grant gradually encircles Lee's troops in the town of Petersburg, Richmond's railway link to the rest of the South.
June 19	The siege of Petersburg begins, lasting for nearly a year until the end of the war.
August 27	General Sherman captures Atlanta and begins the "March to the Sea," a campaign of destruction across Georgia and South Carolina.
November 8	Abraham Lincoln wins reelection, ending hope of the South getting a negotiated settlement.
November 30	Confederate forces are defeated at Franklin, Tennessee, losing five generals. Nashville is soon captured (December 15-16).

1865

April 2	Major Petersburg fortifications fall to the Union, making further resistance by Richmond impossible.
April 3-8	Lee withdraws his army from Richmond and attempts to reach Confederate forces still holding out in North Carolina. Union armies under Grant and Sheridan gradually encircle him.
April 9	Lee surrenders to Grant at Appomattox, Virginia, effectively ending the war.
April 14	Abraham Lincoln is assassinated by John Wilkes Booth, a Southern sympathizer.

Union Army
Army of the Potomac
Army of the James
Army of the Cumberland

Confederate Army
Army of Northern Virginia
Army of Tennessee

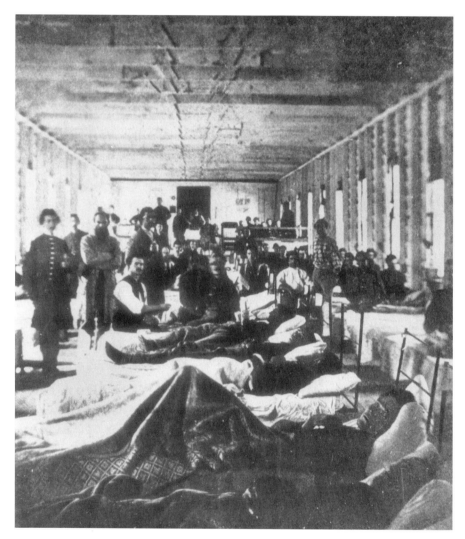

During the Civil War, many brave young men found themselves in military hospitals suffering from serious wounds or equally serious diseases.

I

Building the Confederate Medical Department

*T*wenty-nine years after the American Civil War ended, 24-year-old novelist Stephen Crane had never seen a real war but he wrote one of the most enduring Civil War novels. In *The Red Badge of Courage*, Crane's imaginary soldier, Henry Fleming, is impatient to see his first battle. Crane's pen has Henry think about the battles which he has not yet seen: "The battle was like the grinding of an immense and terrible machine to him. Its complexities and powers, its grim processes, fascinated him. He must go close and see it produce corpses."

When the Civil War began in April 1861, both the Union and the new Confederate States of America had to prepare for war. Neither the South nor the North had any idea of the bloodbath which would flow across the divided country during four bitter, terrible years. Each side believed that the other side would not fight and that the war would end quickly. Neither side predicted the horrendous casualties which would result from the young nation's failure to settle once and for all the hot issues of slavery, the rights of individual states to challenge the legislative will of the national Congress, and the failure to make political peace between the non-slave, industrial North and the pro-slavery, agricultural South. Now only war would settle those issues.

The Confederacy had to build a new country from scratch and build an army and navy out of nothing. The South also had to create a nationwide system for treating all of its sick and wounded soldiers and sailors. The North at least had its prewar army, navy, and military medical department in Washington. These institutions had been improved since 1776. But when war came in 1861, the South had to create its military and its military medical institutions from the ground up.

Confident that Rebel soldiers could defeat the Yankees quickly and cleanly, Southerners in April 1861 could not imagine the flood of sick, wounded, and crippled soldiers which the four-year war would produce. By the war's end in the spring of 1865, on the average, every Southern soldier had been sick or wounded at least six times. Of the approximately 900,000 Confederates who fought for Southern independence, at least 50,000 had been killed or had died from their wounds. And another 150,000 had died from disease. In the North, even more men died in the struggle to conquer the Confederate States of America. But the statistics were similar because the vast majority of Federal dead were killed by disease and not by bullets.

Few of the politicians and strategists in Washington, D.C., or in the Confederate capital of Richmond, Virginia, understood that the American Civil War would be a new kind of war. Even many of the battlefield generals of the North and South did not understand in 1861 that the new rifled musket would make the Civil War the bloodiest war in human history. Generals and politicians still viewed war like their fathers who had fought in the War of 1812, the Mexican War of 1847, or even the Revolutionary War. Few understood that these earlier wars were fought with smoothbore muskets and round, lead bullets like half-inch marbles. These weapons had an effective range of only 100 yards. Effective range is how far away a trained soldier could aim at an enemy soldier and hit him. But the American Civil War introduced rifled muskets which had fine grooves carved inside the rifle's barrel. This groove caused bullets to spin as they left the barrel. Spinning bullets were much more accurate to aim. A rifled musket was deadly with a round ball bullet from 400 yards—four times further than earlier smoothbore muskets.

Then, a French soldier, Captain Claude E. Minié, invented a new kind of bullet for these rifled muskets. His bullet was not a round ball; it was cone-shaped, pointed at the end and wide at its base. The base was hollow and was called a skirt. When the black powder ignited in the rifle barrel, the explosion caused the hollow skirt to expand. The expanding lead skirt was driven into the barrel's grooves and this caused the bullet to spin for accurate aiming. The Minié ball conical bullet was more than half an inch thick and could be aimed at a man 1,000 yards away—and could kill a man even further away. The rifled musket and Minié ball were a revolution in warfare and would cause the wounding and death of thousands of men on Civil War battlefields.

During the first two years of the Civil War, generals in both the North and South failed to understand that the rifled musket and the dreadful Minié ball had changed warfare forever, because both sides at first

Soldiers lie dead or wounded on the battlefield of Gettysburg. The number of wounded and sick soldiers in the war overwhelmed the medical departments of both sides.

used mainly singleshot rifles, which a skilled rifleman could only load and fire two or three times per minute. Neither side understood that famous and glorious charges by thousands of men aligned in neat ranks would now just cause the slaughter of brave men. Once each side learned to build defensive breastworks and trenches on the battlefield to protect their infantry armed with rifled muskets, charging the men behind those breastworks was suicide. Union General Jacob D. Cox recognized that "one rifle in the trench was worth five in front of it." But that did not stop the generals from ordering massed charges by regiments of young soldiers who were then cut to bloody shreds on battlefields like Fredericksburg where most of the dead teenagers wore Yankee blue, or Gettysburg where most of them wore Rebel gray and butternut brown.

During the first 12 major battles of the Civil War, in which total casualties were more than 6,000 men, the Yankees had a total of 809,456 infantrymen in those battles. At least 113,160 of them were killed or wounded—a loss of 14 percent. The Confederates had 622,265 men in those 12 battles of whom 152,841 were casualties—a huge loss of 25 percent. One of these battles was the battle of Antietam, called Sharpsburg in the South. Both sides put a total of 127,000 Americans on that battlefield in Maryland and 23,000 were killed, wounded, or missing after only one day. Antietam remains the bloodiest single day in the history of the United States.

Unlike modern wars where common soldiers, often teenagers and young men, do most of the dying on the battlefield, during the Civil War, officers and even generals were often killed or wounded beside their men. During the 1861-1865 American Civil War, 235 Confederate generals were killed. Half of all Confederate generals were killed or wounded. The new Confederate medical department was hard-pressed to handle these casualities.

The Union and Confederate armies used the regiment as the standard unit of infantry foot soldiers. A regiment was generally 1,000 men, although many regiments were much smaller than that due to losses from battle or disease, when new replacement soldiers were slow in reaching frontline armies. In the Confederacy, at least 42 regiments lost half or more of their men in a single battle. At the July 1863 battle of Gettysburg, 72 percent of the men in the 26th North Carolina Infantry were killed, wounded, or missing. At the September 1862 battle of Antietam, the 1st Texas Regiment lost 82 percent of its men. Such horrendous losses in the war were suffered by the Yankees, too. At Gettysburg, the 1st Minnesota

Regiment lost 85 percent of its men. These were the kinds of losses that surgeons and hospitals had to expect and to treat.

In late February 1861, two months before the war's first shots, the Confederate Congress created the Confederate medical department. Only the Confederate surgeon general, four surgeons, and six assistant surgeons were assigned to the new department for what was expected to be a quick little war. On March 6, 1861, the Congress provided for one surgeon and one assistant surgeon for each Confederate army regiment of volunteer infantrymen. Confederate President Jefferson Davis was given the power to appoint these surgeons. The new medical officers in the new Confederate medical department would wear a standard issue, gray Rebel uniform. A green sash would mark them as physicians since green is the traditional color of the medical profession. Yankee surgeons also wore green on their Federal blue uniforms.

Although the Confederate medical department was created by the Confederate Congress, the department did have men with both medical and military experience. At least 3 surgeons and 21 assistant surgeons assigned to the field were former Yankees who resigned from the United States Army when Civil War came so they could side with the South. The Union Navy also lost 28 to 35 medical officers who joined the Confederacy.

The first Confederate surgeon general was Dr. David C. DeLeon who served only from May 6, 1861, to July 12, 1861. He was replaced by Dr. Charles H. Smith, who only served for the last two weeks of July 1861. The first and final Confederate surgeon general was Dr. Samuel Preston Moore, who served from August 1861 until the war's end. Samuel Moore was a native of Charleston, South Carolina, who had graduated in 1834 from the South Carolina Medical College. Before declaring his loyalty to the Confederacy, Dr. Moore had spent 26 years as a surgeon in the United States Army, which was now his mortal enemy.

From the time of his 1861 appointment to March 1863, Surgeon General Moore served as medical director of all general hospitals and field hospitals. During the war, large general hospitals were built throughout the North and South in each country's larger cities. Closer to the armies which were in constant movement, field hospitals were constructed,

Dr. Samuel Preston Moore served as the Confederate surgeon general for most of the war.

often of nothing more than tents. Army medical officers were the primary physicians and surgeons who remained close to all of the fighting armies. These medical officers were supervised by medical directors. Each medical director served a limited geographical area and supervised the permanent general hospitals and moveable field hospitals within that area. The medical officers reported to their medical directors, and all of the medical directors reported to Surgeon General Moore's headquarters in the Confederate capital city of Richmond, Virginia. This organization of Confederate medicine lasted until March 1863.

On March 12, 1863, the Confederate adjutant general made changes to hospital organization. Each general hospital would now have its own medical director and medical directors would no longer be in charge of the field hospitals within a specific location. Instead, each army would have its own medical director in charge of all of the physicians, surgeons, nurses, and hospital stewards within that army.

The new organization of medical care in the field and close to the fighting began at the regiment level in the army. In each Rebel regiment, one surgeon and one assistant surgeon would handle all of the regiment's medical needs. Two to three regiments made up a brigade. The medical officer in each brigade was a senior surgeon. Three to five brigades formed a division where the chief surgeon was in charge. Two or three divisions in the Confederate army formed a corps where a medical director was in charge. And two to four corps formed an army with all medical staff managed by that army's own medical director. Only the army's medical director would now report directly to the Confederate surgeon general at Richmond.

The lowest level of hospital administration was the hospital steward who was responsible for hospital cleanliness and all supplies. In the Confederacy, hospital stewards were sergeants. Stewards were required to have some knowledge of medications and treatments.

The South had to build its wartime medical system from scratch in 1861, even though there were 21 medical schools in the Confederate States when the war started. During the Civil War, all but one school was closed. The medical school at the University of Virginia stayed open. Its small staff of eight teachers graduated two classes of doctors every year for the duration of the war.

In spite of the dedicated efforts of the Confederate Congress and Dr. Moore to create a useful medical department for Confederate wounded and sick, as the war dragged on and casualties increased, the average Confederate surgeon took care of 324 men at a time. In the North, each Yankee surgeon was responsible for only 133 soldiers, on the average. Throughout the four-year war at least 1,242 military surgeons and 1,994 assistant surgeons served in the Confederate armies. Another 26 military surgeons and 81 assistant surgeons provided medical care to the Confederate navy. The Richmond government also hired hundreds of civilian "contract surgeons" who assisted the military doctors in the army and navy.

When battles left hundreds or thousands of wounded and dying Confederates on the battlefield, the Confederacy's Infirmary Corps was responsible for getting those men off the battlefield and into field hospitals. Generally, only one assistant surgeon and 30 Infirmary Corps men were responsible for taking the wounded off the battlefield. All of these brave men were unarmed and risked their lives if the shooting had not stopped. The Infirmary Corps set up first aid stations very close to the fighting. Here, wounds were quickly dressed in order to move the wounded to field hospitals further from the battle zone. Confederate regulations did not allow soldiers to help their

Dr. Anson Hurd tends to the Confederate wounded after the battle of Antietam in 1862.

Eventually, both sides had to allow women to serve as nurses because of the overwhelming needs of wounded and sick soldiers.

wounded friends and comrades from the battlefield. The North had a similar regulation. The rule was designed to prevent healthy, unhurt soldiers from escaping from the battle by helping the wounded.

During the war's first full year, both sides regarded army doctors as soldiers who could be captured and held as prisoners of war. This policy changed in May 1862 because of one Confederate general. The famous and daring Stonewall Jackson captured eight Yankee medical officers when Confederate troops captured a Union field hospital at Winchester, Virginia, in the Shenandoah Valley. Stonewall Jackson released all eight surgeons and urged them to recommend to President Lincoln that both sides should agree that medical officers would never be captured as prisoners of war.

Within one month, the Yankee's highest ranking general in the field, General George B. McClellan, and Confederate General Robert E. Lee informally agreed between them that all doctors were non-combatants who could not be captured as prisoners of war. That gentleman's agreement became a formal order on the Yankee side by General Order Number 60, which General McClellan signed on June 6, 1862. The Confederate government formalized the agreement with its General Order Number 45, on June 26. Ten months later, on April 24, 1863, the Yankees' General Order Number 100, extended the no-prisoner rule to army chaplains, all medical staff persons, and army nurses.

The Confederacy never had a formal, government-run, nationwide ambulance service for transporting the wounded from the field hospitals to the South's general hospitals. This lack of medical transportation was filled by Richmond's volunteer Ambulance Committee. In the spring of 1862, 100 private citizens organized the Richmond Ambulance Committee. The citizens paid for the horse-drawn ambulances themselves, and these brave volunteers were seen on many battlefields. They were present for most of the great battles fought by Robert E. Lee's Army of Northern Virginia. Just at the May 1863 battle of Chancellorsville, Virginia, these Richmond civilians cared for 7,000 of General Lee's wounded Confederate soldiers.

The Richmond civilian ambulance drivers were not the only civilians actively engaged in the care of sick and wounded Confederates. Throughout the South, women organized private relief agencies which provided clothing, clean bandages, and wholesome food for hungry Rebel armies far from home. These groups called themselves various names such as the Ladies' Soldiers' Aid Society, the Ladies' Soldiers' Relief Society (based in Atlanta), or the Georgia Relief and Hospital Association. The largest such society, and the only one which was nationwide in the Confederacy, was the Association for the Relief of Maimed Soldiers. This organization was formed in January 1864 to buy artificial arms and legs for the tens of thousands of men who had suffered amputations. During the next to the last month of the war, in March 1865, the Confederate Congress, as one of its last official actions, passed a law giving such maimed soldiers free transportation to and from the South's few factories which manufactured artificial limbs.

Wherever these relief societies went, wherever the female nurse matrons went, they saw suffering beyond their worst nightmares. One of the great works of Civil War literature is the diary kept by a southern woman, Mary B. Chesnut. Early in the war, she went to visit the wounded at a Richmond hospital taking fresh fruit for the soldiers. In her diary, she wrote on August 18, 1861: "I went to the hospital with a carriage load of peaches. . . . Those eyes sunk in cavernous depths haunted me as they followed me from bed to bed." For the next three-and-a-half years, it only became worse in Southern hospitals.

Surgeon General Moore set up way hospitals across the South in the spring of 1863. Way hospitals were small buildings along the Confederate railroad lines that provided temporary food and beds for wounded soldiers transported by railroad from battlefields to general hospitals.

The capital city of the Confederacy was also the South's greatest hospital city. Twenty general hospitals were built in Richmond or were made from old warehouses and school buildings. These hospitals were staffed by 43 military surgeons, 65 assistant surgeons, and 18 acting-assistant surgeons who cared for as many as 10,200 sick or wounded Confederates at one time. William A. Carrington spent the war serving as the medical director for all of the Richmond hospitals.

The most famous Confederate general hospital and probably the Civil War's largest general hospital was Chimborazo Hospital in Richmond. It opened in October 1861. Chimborazo was really five separate hospitals working together as one great complex which could treat 8,000 men at one time. Each of the five hospitals at Chimborazo had 30 buildings with beds for 40 to 60 men. Each of these 150 buildings was 100 feet long and 30 feet wide. Five cook houses pro-

duced the hot meals for 8,000 patients. The hospital's own farm cared for 200 cattle used for meat and milk. Two hundred and fifty slaves worked at Chimborazo. The huge hospital's chief was Dr. James Brown McCaw. The son of Superintendent McCaw would become the chief surgeon for all United States forces in Europe during the First World War.

A view of some of the buildings that made up Chimborazo Hospital in Richmond, Virginia.

The next largest hospital in Richmond during the war was Winder General Hospital which opened in April 1862. Six separate hospitals made up Winder, which could treat 5,000 men at one time. Alexander G. Lane was Winder's superintendent.

The number of sick and wounded men who were taken to Richmond could change by the hour, depending upon casualties on battlefields hundreds of miles away. The series of battles between General Robert E. Lee and Yankee General George McClellan in late June 1862 was known as the Seven Days' Campaign. Two great armies pounded each other every day for a week as General Lee pushed the Yankees back from the outskirts of Richmond. During the seven days, more than

Kate Cumming served as a nurse in Confederate hospitals and kept a diary of the pain and suffering she saw.

21,000 wounded Confederates flooded Richmond's general hospitals.

During the entire Civil War, Chimborazo treated 78,000 men and Winder Hospital had 76,000 sick or wounded Confederate patients.

To handle so many sick and wounded men, in September 1862, the Confederate Congress approved the use of female nurses in Southern hospitals. They were called matrons, and two were assigned to each ward in the general hospitals. At the general hospital in Chattanooga, Tennessee, the most famous matron was Kate Cumming who left a diary of her Civil War experience in the ghastly hospitals. On February 21, 1863, Kate wrote in her diary that "many of the patients are brought in at night and are dead before morning."

Another 29 general hospitals were established in Virginia outside of Richmond. These were manned by 56 surgeons, 57 assistant surgeons, and 8 acting-assistant surgeons. As in Richmond, a single battle could overwhelm the state's new general hospitals. A great battle between General Ulysses S. Grant's Federals and Robert E. Lee's Confederates was the battle of the Wilderness in Virginia during May 1864. Three weeks of desperate fighting put 18,000 wounded Confederates in Virginia's hospitals by May 24.

Virginia's hospitals located outside of Richmond saw 114,000 sick and wounded Confederate soldiers between January 1862 and March 1863. Between September 1862 and August 1864, these hospitals reported treating 413,000 men. Just in July 1863, the hospitals in Staunton, Virginia, treated 8,400 sick and wounded men. The Gordonsville, Virginia, general hospital treated 23,642 soldiers from June 1863 to May 1864.

Outside of Virginia, the Confederate state with the most general hospitals was Georgia. Fifty general hospitals were supervised by Dr. Samuel Hollingsworth Stout, an 1848 graduate of the University of Pennsylvania medical school. Confederate hospitals in Tennessee were also part of Dr. Stout's responsibilities. The Georgia and Tennessee hospitals had 7,000 hospital beds for sick and wounded Rebels. Four hospitals in Macon, Georgia, treated 5,000 men during the single year from April 1863 to April 1864.

During the last year of the war, Confederate battlefield casualties were so high that the Richmond government created the Reserve Surgical Corps. Surgeons enjoying the comforts of city life at general hospitals were transferred to war-zone field hospitals to handle the overwhelming number of Confederate casualties.

During four bloody years, Confederate hospitals treated nearly five million Confederate soldiers and sailors. Nearly a quarter million of them died.

Dr. Robert King Stone was one of the doctors who attended to the wounds of Abraham Lincoln. Medical knowledge of the time limited his ability to save the president, as it did many other doctors from saving fallen soldiers in the previous four years.

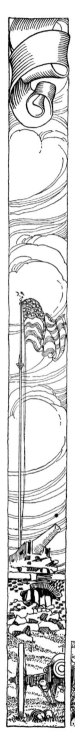
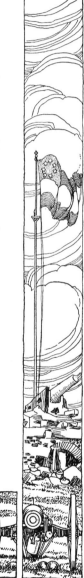

II

Expanding the Federal Medical Department

*U*nlike the new nation of the Confederate States of America, the North did have an existing army and navy with their own medical departments in place since the American Revolution. The North did not have to invent a medical corps, but the prewar medical department had to greatly expand to meet the terrible cost in human suffering caused by the Civil War.

Since the Northern medical departments had been in service for almost a century when civil war erupted in April 1861, the medical services already had traditions of crusty old surgeons managing medical business with great dedication or with petty prejudices. Since the military medical department was based upon rank and seniority, many men had reached positions of power simply by living long—in some cases, too long. Medical minds trained 40 and even 50 years before the Civil War were slow to adapt to its overwhelming casualties and were slower still to listen to younger physicians who brought new ideas and new science to the old medical department. As George

Worthington Adams wrote a century later about the Northern medical department: "Behind the sickness and mortality statistics of the Civil War lie ignorance, stupidity, inefficiency and jealousy. But behind them also . . . are to be seen earnestness, cooperative spirit, and great strides of scientific knowledge which a later generation has all but forgotten."

When the Civil War began, the entire United States Army had only 16,000 men. Their medical needs were met by 30 surgeons and 83 assistant surgeons. After the Southern states left the Union and many army physicians left the Federal army to join the Confederacy, the U. S. Army's medical corps shrank. Within one year, that army of 16,000 men grew to a force of half a million, and would continue growing until the war ended.

At the battle of Fredericksburg, Virginia, in December 1862, Confederate cannons were supervised by Rebel artillery chief Edward Porter Alexander. Just before the Yankees attacked the Confederates' superior position, Alexander remarked to Confederate General James Longstreet that "a chicken could not live on that field when we open on it." Alexander was correct. The Yankee suicide charges left 11,000 Federals dead or wounded under Alexander's batteries of cannon. The Northern medical department had to meet the needs of such horrendous injuries for another two-and-a-half years.

From April 1861 to June 1865, at least 110,070 Federals were killed or died from their wounds. But twice that number—224,586 by one count—died from disease and illness.

Almost two-and-a-half million men served in the Union army and navy during the Civil War. Since many were sick or wounded more than once, the medical department treated 6,454,834 cases of battle

Dorothea Dix was put in charge of the Union's female nurses after they were allowed to serve in the military hospitals.

wounds and camp sickness. At least 6,029,560 of those cases were disease and not wounds. To handle this number of medical cases, the North quickly welcomed female nurses into the medical department. In August 1861, the Federal Congress approved of female matrons and made famous reformer Dorothea Dix superintendent of female matrons. Women were paid 40 cents per day and were provided one meal. Many nurses called their superintendent "Dragon Dix" because of her harsh rules. Dix declared that the women must be older than 30 and must be very plain. Attractive women were not accepted as nurses in the North. They were required to be homely and to know how to cook. Women nurses were not allowed "to go to any place of amusement in the evening." About 3,200 women volunteered as Yankee nurses. One of

Dix's unwritten rules was that her nurses should be Protestant; Catholics were not welcome, although hundreds of Catholic nuns worked heroically in Federal hospitals throughout the war.

The crusty old doctors of the prewar army ran the medical department for the war's first year. Not until the spring of 1862 did the Federal government actively look for new men with new ideas. On April 16, 1862, Abraham Lincoln signed a Congressional act which reorganized the prewar medical department. The army's assistant surgeon general, Dr. William Alexander Hammond, became the new surgeon general of the United States. The budget for the medical department was increased from $2.4 million in 1862 to $11.6 million in 1863. Old military surgeons who had survived because of the army's seniority system were replaced by younger doctors. Many of Surgeon General Hammond's proposals for modernizing the medical corps met with angry opposition from army surgeons and from congressmen who did not like changes. The revolutionary legislation also created the new post of medical inspector which authorized inspectors to examine field hospitals and general hospitals for efficiency and quality of medical care.

Unlike the Confederacy, which had only private soldier relief societies with little or no real power, the United States government recognized the need for civilian advisors on medical issues. During the war's first two months, the Women's

Dr. William A. Hammond was appointed the Federal surgeon general in 1862.

Central Association of Relief in New York City sent a delegation to Washington to lobby President Lincoln to create a national relief agency with power to make recommendations to the government for medical care of wounded and sick Union soldiers. On June 18, 1861, President Lincoln created the United States Sanitary Commission, which would play a vital role in medical care during the war. Although started by New York City women, there were no women in the Sanitary Commission's upper levels. Lincoln approved Reverend Henry W. Bellows as commission president and Frederick Law Olmstead—a landscape architect who designed New York City's Central Park—as the commission's general secretary. Twenty-one commissioners were appointed. Three of the commissioners were soldiers.

Reverend Henry Bellows headed the U.S. Sanitary Commission during the Civil War. The Sanitary Commission worked tirelessly to help improve medical care for the Union's soldiers.

The Sanitary Commission grew quickly and chapters were active in 2,500 Northern cities and towns. In the West, an independent Western Sanitary Commission based at St. Louis, Missouri, did the job of the U. S. Sanitary Commission in that area.

U. S. Surgeon General Hammond worked to modernize the medical department. In December 1862, Congress approved Hammond's recommendation to increase the number of medical inspectors and to raise the military rank of surgeons from major to lieutenant colonel. But in January 1863, Congress refused Dr. Hammond's request to increase the food allowance for sick and wounded soldiers from 18 cents per day to 30 cents. But Congress did approve Dr. Hammond's request for 50 more surgeons and 250 more assistant surgeons for the army medical department.

Dr. Hammond also saw the need for a formal, nationwide ambulance corps for transporting wounded soldiers from the battlefield to distant hospitals. He recommended the creation of an army postgraduate medical school to assure that surgeons were aware of the latest developments in medical science. In 1863, the secretary of war turned down both of these requests. On his own, Dr. Hammond asked surgeons traveling with the army to submit medical papers and specimens for a future U. S. Army Medical Museum. The surgeon general also created the army's first microbiology department to study the little-known bodies called bacteria.

In August 1861, Dr. Charles S. Tripler became the medical director for the Army of the Potomac which did battle with Robert E. Lee's Confederates for three bloody years. Under Dr. Tripler's reforms, a detailed medical chain of command was created in General George McClellan's army. Regimental surgeons reported to brigade surgeons; a medical director would serve at the division level. Brigade surgeons were given responsibility for inspecting army camp sanitation, managing medical supplies, and collecting doctors' reports and casualty numbers after battles.

During the first months of the war, the real enemy of the military medical departments was not battle wounds; the enemy was sickness. In October 1861, the Yankees' Army of the Potomac had 133,000 men poised to invade Virginia. Of these troops, at least 19,000 were sick. By July 1862, after the Seven Days' Campaign around Richmond, the Army of the Potomac was down to 89,000 healthy soldiers with 55,000 men either wounded, dead, or sick. Unfortunately, Confederate medical records are incomplete, and many Confederate government documents were destroyed as the war was coming to an end in 1865. What Richmond medical records did survive show that between July 1861 and March 1862, the Confederate forces in Virginia suffered 148,000 cases of disease or illness.

The Seven Days' Campaign which ended on July 1, 1862, left 2,980 Federals killed and 13,000 wounded. Just as that battle forced Richmond to accommodate 21,000 Rebel wounded, the North also had to adjust to a flood of wounded men larger than ever before.

The North's field hospitals in the countryside were regimental hospitals, with wounded men treated at their own regiment's tent hospitals close to the battlefield. Each Federal regiment in 1861 was assigned three large wall-tents which were 15 feet long, 14 feet wide, and 11 feet tall. The sides were upright for the first few feet in wall tents. Regimental field hospitals also included one Sibley tent resembling a tall tepee, and one common tent with sloping sides, a single horizontal pole through the top, and open ends.

Dr. Tripler tried to remedy the lack of ambulance drivers and medics in the Army of the Potomac. During the first year of the war, the members of each regiment's band served as that regiment's battlefield first-aid men. Fifteen musicians and 10 soldiers were assigned to each regiment as stretcher-bearers to assist the wounded. Each regiment was also assigned two kinds of ambulances, one four-wheeled and one two-wheeled. These wagons belonged to the army's Quartermaster Corps and not to the medical department. By October 1861, 119 of 228 two-wheeled ambulances were already broken-down or missing.

In October 1861, the U. S. Sanitary Commission inspected the Army of the Potomac and reported to Washington that 105 regimental field hospitals were

33

Dr. Jonathan Letterman served as medical director for the North's Army of the Potomac. He worked to form an ambulance corps to transport wounded and sick soldiers from the battlefields.

rated as good, 52 were rated only as tolerable, and 26 were "bad."

The Sanitary Commission was largely supported by private donations from Northern civilians. The commission held sanitary fairs across the country to raise money. The first fair was held at Lowell, Massachusetts, in February 1863. The largest fair was held in October 1863 at Chicago. Auctions were held to finance the Commission's work. President Lincoln donated the original draft of his Emancipation Proclamation to the Chicago fair for auction. It was sold for $3,000. The Chicago fair brought in $79,000. During the four years of war, the commission raised $5,000,000 and collected $15,000,000 worth of medical supplies.

Three days after the battle of Seven Days, in 1862, Dr. Jonathan Letterman replaced Dr. Tripler as the medical director for the Army of the Potomac.

Dr. Letterman's first political battle for reforming army medicine was a nearly two-year effort to create a formal, government ambulance corps for transporting wounded men from the battle zone—something the Confederacy never created. He tried first to take the ambulance operation away from regimental bands and to create trained medics. In August 1862, General George McClellan issued General Order Number 147, which adopted Dr. Letterman's idea for an ambulance corps. At the army corps level, a captain was put in charge of army ambulances; a first lieutenant was put in charge of division ambulances; a second lieutenant was put in charge of brigade ambulances; and, at the regiment level, a sergeant was in charge. Each regiment was assigned one four-horse ambulance and two two-horse ambulances. General McClellan's order did include a provision similar to the Confederacy's Infirmary Corps restrictions on removing the wounded during a battle: "No person will be allowed to carry from the field any wounded or sick except this [ambulance] corps." The order did not require any special training for the ambulance men.

Dr. Letterman's ambulance system was first tested in the horrific battle of Antietam on September 17, 1862. His 300 ambulances performed well. Within one day, they removed 10,000 Federal wounded from the battlefield and moved them to 71 field hospitals. One month after General McClellan's order, on October 30, 1862, Dr. Letterman reorganized the entire hospital organization for the Army of the Potomac.

Dr. Letterman established division hospitals with a new delegation of medical duties: one assistant surgeon from each regiment was assigned to frontline wound-dressing stations very close to the battlefield. Division hospitals took over the duties of regimental

A line of ambulance wagons and drivers wait at Harewood Hospital in Washington, D.C.

Wounded soldiers await transport after the battle of Fredericksburg.

hospitals. At the division hospital level, one army medical officer was assigned the duty of keeping accurate hospital records, another medical officer was given the responsibility of managing medical supplies, and only one of every 15 medical officers was assigned to full-time surgery duties. The new organization of medical officers was tested on December 13, 1862, at the battle of Fredericksburg, Virginia. Division hospitals and the new ambulance corps performed well in handling the 9,000 Federal wounded.

Dr. Letterman's reorganization of division hospitals was also applied to the Union armies fighting in the West. During General Ulysses Grant's two-month siege of Vicksburg, Mississippi, division hospitals and the new ambulance corps system were used. Field hospitals were helped by the hospitals of Memphis, Tennessee, which had beds for 5,000 wounded Federals.

At the greatest battle of the war, the three-day battle of Gettysburg during July 1-3, 1863, the newest medical reorganization was tested: 650 medical officers with 1,000 horse-drawn ambulances manned by 3,000 ambulance corps drivers and medics performed better than expected. Most Union casualties were removed from the terrible battlefield within one day. By the Fourth of July 1863, more than 14,000 Federal wounded had been removed to division hospital tents. When the Army of the Potomac left Pennsylvania to pursue Robert E. Lee's retreating Confederate army, 106 Union medical officers were left behind at Gettysburg to care for the 21,000 Yankee and Rebel wounded who were too badly hurt to be moved.

Not until August 24, 1863, did the United States Army require examinations for ambulance drivers to test their knowledge of first aid. New green stripes for uniforms were given to the men who passed their tests.

In the fall of 1863, U. S. Surgeon General Hammond continued to urge reforms in the army's medical corps. His outspoken opinions made him many political enemies. He had a reputation for being impatient with politicians and older army officers who were slow to accept new ways of caring for sick and wounded soldiers. Hammond insisted that his medical inspectors—a job he had created—should be appointed for their merit. The politicians and senior officers wanted inspectors appointed for political reasons. In November 1863, Dr. Hammond had offended enough powerful people that he was removed from office. By December, Dr. Joseph K. Barnes had replaced Dr. Hammond as surgeon general. Barnes served for the rest of the war. He went on to adopt many of Dr. Hammond's reforms, including the creation of an Army Medical Museum and Army Medical Library. When Dr. Hammond lost his job, Dr. Letterman of the

Dr. Joseph K. Barnes served as U.S. surgeon general after Dr. Hammond was removed from office.

Army of the Potomac was also fired since he had so often agreed with Dr. Hammond's reforms.

Although removed from the Army of the Potomac, Dr. Letterman's reforms were continued by Lieutenant General Grant who was made Union general-in-chief in the spring of 1864. Although General George Gordon Meade, given command of the Army of the Potomac shortly before Gettysburg, remained that army's commander on paper, Grant is thought of as the real commander since his headquarters became part of Meade's army.

General Grant's first great battle with the Army of the Potomac was the battle of the Wilderness in Virginia during the first week of May 1864. Grant fought General Lee's Army of Northern Virginia every single day for the next six weeks. Between May 5 and July 31, 1864, Grant's Union casualties overwhelmed the medical department. The army suffered the loss of 46,000 wounded men and 11,000 sick soldiers. Seven thousand wounded were evacuated just from the Wilderness battlefield. Army ambulances followed within five miles of the advancing Army of the Potomac, instead of the usual 25 miles as they had done on the road to Gettysburg. There were so many Union wounded in so short a time that a large hospital was established at the Union base of Fredericksburg, Virginia. Six thousand wounded were moved to Fredericksburg after the May 12, 1864, battle of Spotsylvania, Virginia. There were only 40 army surgeons for the wounded at Fredericksburg's hospitals. During the campaign, Grant used Dr. Letterman's division hospital system with each division assigned 14 supply wagons and 4 medical wagons. The medical wagons carried 22 hospital tents and medicines.

The political battle in the North for creating an army-wide ambulance corps had begun with Dr.

Letterman in 1862. It continued for another two years with the help of Dr. Henry I. Bowditch of Boston. His son had been killed at the Second Battle of Bull Run in August 1862. Bowditch went to Washington to urge then-Surgeon General Hammond to create a formal ambulance corps for all Union armies. Then Dr. Bowditch made the same plea to General Henry Halleck and General George McClellan. General McClellan agreed with Dr. Hammond, but General Halleck objected and nothing was done.

In February 1863, Dr. Bowditch took his idea to the United States Congress.

After Dr. Henry Bowditch's son was killed at the Second Battle of Bull Run, he worked tirelessly to create a formal ambulance corps.

The U.S. Sanitary Commission agreed with Dr. Bowditch and asked for 12,000 men for the United States Ambulance Corps. When General Halleck and War Secretary Edwin Stanton both opposed the bill, Congress failed to pass it. Not until March 1864, the beginning of the war's last year, did Congress finally pass the Ambulance Corps Bill which created an ambulance corps to serve all Union armies. The bill continued General McClellan's order that only ambulance corps medics could remove wounded men from the battlefield. The ambulance corps was modeled after the plans of Dr. Hammond and Drs. Tripler and Letterman—all men who had lost their jobs for being too aggressive in demanding better medical care for Union soldiers. The new law also finally required examinations for ambulance corps men which had not been part of General McClellan's earlier order creating an informal ambulance corps in August 1862.

When he was medical director for the Army of the Potomac, Dr. Charles Tripler was a reformer in many areas of medical care. But he did not believe in general hospitals. "I consider general hospitals nuisances," he wrote to General McClellan on February 7, 1863, "to be tolerated only because there are occasions when they are absolutely necessary." Dr. Tripler's main objection was that general hospitals removed men from the army. "A leading object with me," he wrote, "was to keep up the fighting force to its maximum and therefore . . . I discouraged the practice of sending them to the general hospitals."

But in the North as in the South, wounded and sick soldiers by the tens of thousands simply overwhelmed field and division-level tent hospitals. General hospitals had to be built throughout the North as in the South. Northern general hospitals treated 1,057,523 patients during the war.

The blacks serving in the United States Army were generally denied access to these big-city general hospitals. Most northern blacks and freed Southern slaves who served in the Union army were in the United States Colored Troops regiments. In 1990, University of Houston, Texas, historian Joseph T. Glatthaar called Federal medical treatment of blacks "woeful and discriminatory medical care." The 178,000 blacks in the Union armies saw action in hundreds of different battles. But they never enjoyed the same standard of medical care as white Northern soldiers. This was especially true at general hospitals. As Professor Glatthaar has noted, "[G]eneral hospitals which cared for seriously ill patients, regularly had separate and grossly unequal facilities for Blacks. . . . [D]eath rates [for Blacks] were dramatically higher than in adjacent or nearby facilities for whites." At the Union general hospitals at Vicksburg, Mississippi, captured by General Grant in July 1863, there was a general hospital for whites and a separate hospital for blacks. At the hospital for whites, 14 percent of the patients died. But at the hospital for Union black soldiers, 30 percent died.

The first Union general hospital was built at Parkersburg, West Virginia, in early 1862. It had two wooden wards, each 130 feet long and 25 feet wide. The ceiling was built 14 feet high to provide good ventilation.

Among the largest general hospitals was Harewood Hospital in Washington. It was created so quickly to accept the wounded from the battle of Antietam that Harewood started as a huge complex of canvas tents with room for 3,000 men. By July 1862, Washington had 6,000 beds for wounded and sick Yankees. Only two months later, there were beds for 20,000 men. Between September 1862 and January 1863, Washington hospitals treated 56,000 men. During May 1864, General Grant's battle of the Wilderness sent 26,000 men to Washington's general hospitals.

By the end of the war, there were 16 general hospitals in Washington. By 1864, Union general hospitals

Hospital tents were set up at the rear of Douglas Hospital in Washington, D.C., to house the over-flow of wounded and sick soldiers.

in Nashville, Memphis, and Chattanooga, Tennessee, had beds for 24,500 Federals. The city of Philadelphia had 27 general hospitals with beds for 25,000 men by the war's end. Small Northern cities also had general hospitals. The hospital at Jeffersonville, Indiana, had 2,600 beds by early 1864.

General hospitals were built throughout the North to meet rising casualties. There were 28,000 hospital beds available for Union sick and wounded in the North by August 1862. By November, there were 56,000 beds. By June 1863, the North's 182 general hospitals had beds for 84,000 soldiers and sailors. One year later, 190 hospitals had beds for 121,000 men. And by the time the war ended, 204 Union general hospitals had room for 137,000 men at one time.

To serve the Union sick and wounded, some 12,000 surgeons served the Federal medical department between 1861 and 1865. These doctors included 2,109 surgeons and 3,882 assistant surgeons attached to infantry regiments. All of them were appointed by the state governors where each regiment was raised. Another 5,532 surgeons were civilian "contract surgeons" hired by the army without military rank. Contract surgeons worked for $90 per month if they served full-time. Part-time contract surgeons were paid $30 per month. Just as black Union soldiers were generally denied access to general hospitals, even their surgeons had to be specially appointed. President Lincoln appointed all of the surgeons assigned to the United States Colored Troops regiments.

Often the surgeons, military or contract, were too close to the battlefield for their own safety. But they continued to bravely serve the sick and wounded. During the war, among Northern doctors, 42 were killed, 83 were wounded, 290 died from diseases or injuries, and 4 died as prisoners of war despite the pledges of both sides not to take physicians prisoner.

But as we've said, although shot and shell killed at least 94,000 Confederates and 110,000 Federals, the real enemies of doctors in both the North and South were disease and infection. Army doctors on both sides treated a total of 400,000 wounds. But they treated six million cases of disease—and disease almost always won.

Hundreds of Catholic nuns served tirelessly in the hospitals of the Civil War.

III

The Battle Against Disease

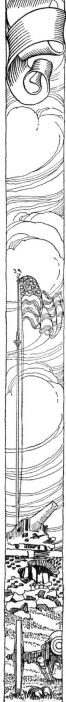

A century after the American Civil War, Dr. Paul Steiner of the University of Pennsylvania's School of Medicine, Department of Pathology, said of the war: "Microbes had nearly all the advantages."

As with most Civil War medical statistics, the records for the North are much more complete than those of the South. Also, most Northern records were kept only for white soldiers. Generally, Yankees suffered disease and illness at the rate of 2,435 cases for every 1,000 men—this means than most soldiers were sick at least twice. Union blacks suffered 3,299 illness cases for every 1,000 black soldiers—figures which reflect the inferior medical care received by black Federals. Disease killed 53 of every 1,000 white Federals and 143 of every 1,000 black Federals. Ninety percent of black Northern soldiers who died were killed by disease and not by battle. Of 178,000 northern blacks who wore Yankee blue, at lease 29,000 died from disease. The most common diseases were diarrhea and dysentery for which separate statistics were

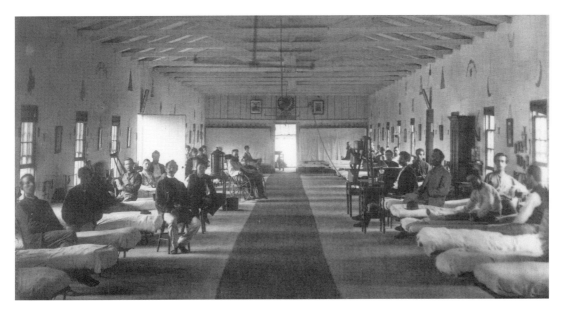

Patients at Armory Square Hospital in Washington, D.C.

not kept. The Union troops suffered these illnesses at the rate of 711 cases for each 1,000 men.

In the North, slightly more than 67,000 men were killed on the battlefield and another 43,000 died later from wounds. But 224,586 Yankees died from disease. Many Union regiments lost far more men to disease than to Rebel bullets. The single highest death rate from disease for Yankees was suffered by the 65th United States Colored Troops Regiment, which lost 755 men killed by disease and no men killed in battle. The 5th Colorado Artillery Regiment had 701 men die from disease and 128 killed in battle. In the 2nd Tennessee Infantry, disease killed 613 men but only 27 were killed in battle. The 6th Michigan Infantry saw 502 men die of disease and 78 killed in battle. And the 32nd Missouri Infantry had 414 men killed by disease and only 20 killed in battle.

Union medical statistics did not separate "soldiers' diarrhea" from dysentery because Civil War medicine did not recognize that diarrhea is generally a symptom of some other disease or infection, while dysentery is a separate, killer disease of the intestines caused by microscopic bacteria or parasites. Federal records lumped the two into one category.

The greatest killer of Union soldiers and sailors was the diarrhea/dysentery combination. They struck fully 1.7 million men and killed 44,558. The next most common disease was malaria which infected 1.3 million Yankees and killed 10,063. The worst killer of men after diarrhea/dysentery was typhoid fever. Although only 149,000 Federals caught typhoid, it killed 34,833. Pneumonia struck 77,000 Federals and killed 19,971. Today, measles is regarded as a childhood disease which has been virtually eradicated in all developed countries. But measles was a killer of many adults during the Civil War. At least 76,000 Federals caught measles and 5,177 of them died. Tuberculosis struck 29,500 Yankees and killed 6,946. And smallpox killed another 7,000 Union men.

The terrible disease and sickness rates among Northern soldiers began with their first day in the army. When Dr. Tripler was medical director for the

These tents served as a general hospital in City Point, Virginia, during the siege of Petersburg in 1864.

Army of the Potomac, the army's General Order Number 51, of August 31, 1861, required a thorough physical examination of new recruits volunteering to enter the army. That order was generally ignored and sickly volunteers joined the Union army in large numbers. As Dr. Tripler wrote in February 1863, "I doubt whether this most important order has ever received the slightest attention. . . . The effect of this neglect, incompetency, or dishonesty, has been always to swell essentially the ratio of the sick to the whole force."

With sickly men enlisting in the Union armies, by May 1861, at least 30 percent of the army in the East was already sick. That percentage continued for the next four months. Between November 1861 and October 1862 just in South Carolina, Union soldiers suffered 12,000 cases of dysentery, 3,800 cases of malaria, 3,200 cases of fevers, at least 3,000 cases of bronchitis, more than 1,670 cases of typhoid fever, and 749 cases of measles. In West Virginia during the two months ending in September 1861, the Union army listed 20,000 sick men, of whom 150 died.

The most historically interesting outbreak of Civil War disease occurred at Corinth, Mississippi, between April and June 1862. This was the only military campaign which was defeated strictly by disease. Confederate troops commanded by General Pierre G. Beauregard held Corinth with 112,000 Rebel soldiers. Nearby at Shiloh, Tennessee, General Grant's Yankees numbered only 90,000. General Beauregard's army was completely crippled by disease. Out of an army counted at 112,000 Confederates, at least 28,000 men were sent home or to general hospitals to recover from sickness. Another 26,000 troops were listed as sick at Corinth. With his Southern army reduced by disease to only 53,000 healthy men, Beauregard abandoned Corinth to the Yankees on May 19. Disease had won a major victory for Ulysses S. Grant. During seven weeks of sickness, disease had killed as many Confederates at Corinth as Yankee guns had killed in April at the vicious battle of Shiloh, Tennessee.

Diseases at prison camps were especially severe in both the North and South. At the war's most infamous prison, Camp Sumter at Andersonville, Georgia, the prison hospital treated 17,875 sick Union prisoners of war. More than 11,000 of them died.

The primary causes of Civil War disease were poor sanitation at hospitals and in army camps. The primary cause of the ineffective treatments for diseases and infections was simply the limited scientific knowledge of the 1860s. The entire United States Army during the civil war had only 20 medical thermometers. The headquarters of the army's medical department did not receive its first microscope until 1863—halfway through the war. But the lack of medical equipment which is taken for granted today was not limited to the army medical departments. Harvard University's medical school did not get its first stethoscope until three years after the Civil War ended, and its first microscope arrived four years after the war.

Treatments for disease and infection were nearly unknown to the doctors and surgeons of both sides. The most common dangerous disease to Union and Confederate soldiers was dysentery. It killed almost as many men as were killed in action on the battlefields. During the first 18 months of the Civil War, 25 percent of all sick Confederate soldiers east of the Mississippi River suffered from diarrhea or dysentery. At Richmond's Chimborazo Hospital, 20 percent of all patients suffered from dysentery during 1861 and 1862. No one knew that true dysentery was caused by bacteria or parasites. The Union doctors treated dysentery with concoctions of castor oil mixed with

Dr. Jonathan Letterman (seated on left) is shown with his staff in November 1862.

opium. Confederate doctors preferred acetate of lead with opium.

No one knew that malaria and yellow fever were caused by bites from one specific kind of mosquito. Malaria was worse in Southern coastal areas. From January 1862 to July 1863 in South Carolina, Georgia, and Florida, Yankees soldiers suffered 14,842 cases of malaria and Confederate troops suffered 41,539 cases. During this same 19-month period, Confederate troops at Mobile, Alabama, reported 13,668 malaria cases. By the end of the war, at least one million Yankees had malaria.

Civil War doctors did know that the chemical quinine could control malaria, but it couldn't cure the disease completely. The Union doctors prescribed quinine by the barrels. Southern doctors also used quinine while their supply lasted. When supplies were low, Confederate medical officers prescribed useless combinations of tincture of dogwood, poplar, and willow tree bark—mixed with whiskey.

Yellow fever was sometimes brought to the South from foreign countries when ships tried to break through the Yankee naval blockade of Southern seaports to bring to the South weapons, food, and medical equipment. The steamship *Kate* ran the Union blockade from Nassau in the Bahama Islands. The ship made it to Wilmington, North Carolina, on August 6, 1862, carrying an unseen and deadly cargo of either sailors infected with yellow fever or mosquitos carrying the disease. A Wilmington dock worker was the first civilian to die from yellow fever on September 9. By November 1862, the city had 1,500 cases of yellow fever. Seven hundred civilians eventually died from the disease.

Typhoid fever accounted for only 2 percent of all Union illnesses. But typhoid was deadly and accounted for one-fourth of all deaths from disease among Northern soldiers. It also killed one-fourth of all Confederates who died from disease. Between January 1862 and April 1863, the Confederacy had 4,749 typhoid cases just in Virginia outside of the Richmond area. Of these, 1,619 died. Richmond's Chimborazo Hospital treated 1,388 typhoid cases during the war, of whom 661 died. The death rates from

These buildings and tents served as a field hospital during the battle of Fair Oaks.

typhoid actually increased as the war dragged on. In the Union armies in 1861, 17 percent of typhoid patients died. But by 1865, more than half died. Medical treatments were useless: the North tried quinine, opium, whiskey, and turpentine mixtures. The South relied upon turpentine oil.

Pneumonia was especially deadly. No one knew the difference between pneumonia caused by bacteria or viruses. One-fourth of all Confederates who died from disease died from pneumonia, about 20,000 men. During one 19-month period in 1861-1862, 17 percent of Confederate soldiers had pneumonia and nearly 20 percent of those died. Physicians in both the North and South treated the disease with heat applied to the chest.

Finally, smallpox killed almost half of its victims. In Virginia alone from October 1, 1862, to January 31, 1864, there were 2,513 smallpox patients in general hospitals of whom 1,020 died. In Richmond during the single week between December 12, 1862, and December 19, there were 250 cases of whom 110 died.

Civil War medicine for disease was primitive and deadly. By the time of the next great modern war, the First World War, medical advances would have seemed like miracles to Civil War doctors. As George Worthington Adams wrote: "[C]enturies, not a mere two generations, might well have separated 1865 and 1914."

IV

The Perils of Dirty Knives and Bone Saws

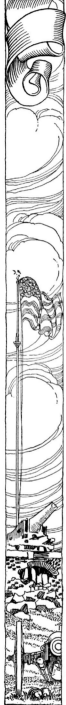

*I*f Civil War disease and sickness were deadly, Civil War surgery was a horror of blood, pain, and what surgeons cheerfully called "laudable pus."

Battlefield wounds which required hospitalization or surgery were dreaded by all soldiers of the Civil War. In July 1864, Yankee Private Robert Hale Strong of the 105th Illinois Volunteer Infantry spent time at the Chattanooga, Tennessee, general hospital. He remembered: "One day the sergeant in charge of our ward asked me to go to the next tent with him to see them dress the wounds of a certain badly wounded man. This man was hit in the left side. The shell had cut away a portion of his side, ribs and all. When his wound was exposed for dressing, one could see his heart beat."

The Union armies suffered 250,000 bullet wounds of which 14 percent were fatal. Statistics for Northern soldiers show that 71 percent of all bullet wounds

were in the arms and legs, which accounted for so many amputations. Eighteen percent of wounds were in the torso and 11 percent were in the head or neck.

The rifled musket with its 1,000-yard deadly accuracy could shoot round lead balls or the conical Minié ball. Because the lead of both bullets was soft, bullets tended to deform and flatten when they entered soldiers' bodies. Deformed bullets ripped through organs and shattered bones. Nearly all abdominal wounds which struck the small intestines were fatal. If the large intestines alone were damaged, 40 percent of these wounds were fatal. Any bullet which pierced the stomach was regarded as 100 percent fatal. A liver wound was also 100 percent fatal. Chest wounds which tore lung tissue were 62 percent fatal. And a wound to the pelvis and hip area killed the wounded man 80 percent of the time.

Surgeons work on wounded soldiers at the rear of a battlefield.

The single greatest cause of death on the battlefield was loss of blood or hemorrhage. In 1861, there was no such thing as a blood or plasma transfusion. Lost blood was blood lost forever. Civil War doctors classified hemorrhage in three ways: primary hemorrhage occurred with the wound and over the next 24 hours; intermediary hemorrhage occurred between the first and sixth days after the wound; and secondary hemorrhage occurred between days four and ten after the injury. Generally, the 10th day after being wounded was the day of highest risk for hemorrhage (secondary) and death. This was caused by infection attacking the body's blood vessels until they weaken and leak.

Although no one really understood germs and infection during the war, at least there was anesthesia for surgery. But many surgeons argued against anesthesia and putting men to sleep for surgery. They believed that anesthesia slowed healing and increased blood loss during surgery. Many believed that profound pain prevented dangerous shock after blood loss. Fortunately, most surgeons did use anesthesia. Ether had been in use since 1846 and chloroform since 1851. In some 80,000 Union operations for wounds when anesthesia was used, 76 percent of the operations used chloroform to put the wounded patient to sleep, 14 percent used ether, and 9 percent used a mixture of the two chemicals. Surgeons preferred chloroform since it did not burn or explode like ether could.

At least 30,000 wounded Yankees suffered amputations of legs or arms by surgeons who did not know to wash their hands or their instruments before operating. Private Strong remembered the result of amputations: "Near the hospital was a pile of arms, legs, hands, and feet that had been cut from the wounded. These had not been buried, just thrown in a pile, and

Wounded soldiers lie on the ground awaiting care at a field hospital in June of 1862.

worms had begun to work on them." These scenes of horror were the same in the South.

Surgeons classified amputations similarly to hemorrhage. A primary amputation occurred during the first 24 hours after a bone-shattering wound to an arm or leg. Secondary amputations occurred after the first day. These were the most dangerous. At Richmond's general hospitals from June 1 to August 1, 1862, there were 272 primary amputations with 82 of the patients dying. But of 308 secondary amputations, more than half died. From April 1861 to October 1864 in Richmond hospitals, there were 1,142 primary amputations with 315 deaths, and 546 secondary amputations with 284 deaths.

Confederate nurse Kate Cumming watched the amputations at the Corinth, Mississippi, hospital on April 23, 1862: "The amputating table for this ward is

at the end of the hall, near the landing of the stairs . . . I was compelled to pass the place. . . . A stream of blood ran from the table into a tub in which was an arm. It had been taken off at the socket, and the hand . . . was hanging over the edge of the tub."

In all Civil War hospitals, infection after surgery was often a death sentence. None of the country's leading physicians could agree on what precisely caused wounds to become infected. The microscope had been in use for 200 years, and microbes unseen to the naked eye were known since 1665 when Robert Hooke published his treatise, "Micrographia." But the precise relationship between germs and infection was not known. Indeed, white pus oozing from a three- or four-day-old wound was regarded as a very good sign that a wound was healing. Surgeons were so pleased to see it that they called it "laudable pus." That this pus meant inflammation and infection from potentially deadly Staphylococcus aureus bacteria was unknown.

The deadliest hospital infection was pyemia—pus in the blood stream, now usually called bacteremia. Pyemia was caused by streptococcal pyogenic bacteria and it killed 97 percent of its Civil War victims. Tetanus caused by wounds contaminated with battle-field soil killed 89 percent of its patients. To this day, no modern scientist is certain as to which bacteria might have caused the terrifying Civil War infection known as hospital gangrene. There were 2,600 cases of hospital gangrene in Northern hospitals. Writing a century later, George Worthington Adams described hospital gangrene this way: "The gangrene patient might see a black spot the size of a dime appear on his healing wound, and watch with horrified interest its rapid spread until his whole leg or arm was but a rotten, evil-smelling mass of dead flesh."

Civil War surgeons may not have known the causes of inflammation and infection, but they did know from experience that some chemicals seemed to slow the spread of infection or even to stop it. These were effective antiseptics, although antibiotics like penicillin were still 60 years into the future. Doctors could even treat some hospital gangrene by cutting away the dead flesh and cleaning the wound with a bromine solution—if the patient and his doctor could tolerate bromine's suffocating fumes. The cleaned wound was then packed with lint soaked in a weak bromine solution. Only 3 percent of the patients treated early with bromine died. With other antiseptics, 38 percent died.

Although antiseptic agents were known, they were often not effective since surgeons tended to wait far too long before resorting to them. Common antiseptics used with some effectiveness were carbolic acid, chlorine, powdered charcoal, sodium hypochlorite, and bichloride of mercury. How or why they worked, no one knew.

These doctors served with the 4th Division, Ninth Corps, at the siege of Petersburg.

★ ★ ★

Wounded soldiers outside a hospital at Fredericksburg, Virginia, in 1864.

For those four bloody, agonizing years of national tragedy, the history of Civil War medicine was truly the story of each individual sick or wounded soldier suffering one at a time, far from his home and family. Private Robert Hale Strong watched one of these struggles at his Chattanooga hospital in July 1864:

He had been shot clear through the head, the ball entering just under the eye and coming out at the back of his head. The doctor took a silk rag, oiled it, threaded it into a long silver needle, and pushed the needle through the boy's head. He drew the silk rag after it and brought out three or four great big maggots. He repeated this several times.

Thus was rudimentary medicine practiced on the hundreds of thousands of soldiers who were carried from the battlefields and army camps of the Civil War. The surgeons and doctors were for the most part caring, competent men, but knowledgeable only to a certain point—their hands tied by the lack of medical knowledge in their century. So soldiers died, limbs were cut off, and no one knew how to save them. After the war, over a million veterans limped home with healed or half-healed wounds and with lingering infections and diseases which would cripple them for life.

Glossary

bluecoats	Term used for soldiers in the Northern Union army during the Civil War because of the color of their uniforms.
Confederacy	The Confederate States of America; the South.
Confederate	Citizen of the Confederate States of America; a Southerner during the Civil War.
dysentery	A disease of the intestines caused by bacteria, characterized by severe diarrhea.
Federals	A name used for members of the Union.
field hospitals	Hospital areas, usually in tents, set up close to army camps.
graycoats	Term used for soldiers in the Southern Confederate army during the Civil War because of the color of their uniforms.
malaria	A disease transmitted by mosquitos characterized by chills and fever.
Rebels	Term used for Southerners in the Civil War.
rifled muskets	A single-shot rifle with grooves (rifling) in the barrel that propelled bullets farther than smoothbore muskets.
steward	Person responsible for cleanliness and supplies in a military hospital.
typhoid fever	A contagious disease that involves high fever, headache, diarrhea, and inflammation of the intestines.
Union	The United States of America; the North.
way hospitals	Hospitals set up along transportation lines to care for wounded soldiers as they were being transported to general hospitals.
Yankees	Term used for Northerners during the Civil War.

Further Reading

Adams, George Worthington. *Doctors in Blue*. Dayton, Ohio: Morningside, 1985.

Chesnut, Mary Boykin. *A Diary from Dixie*, Ben Ames Williams, ed. Cambridge: Harvard University, 1980.

Cumming, Kate. *Kate: The Journal of a Confederate Nurse*, Richard B. Harwell, ed. Baton Rouge: Louisiana State University Press, 1959.

Cunningham, H. H. *Doctors in Gray: The Confederate Medical Service*. Baton Rouge: Louisiana State, 1958.

Freemon, Frank R. *Gangrene and Glory: Medical Care during the American Civil War*. Cranbury, NJ: Associated University Press, 1998.

Steiner, Paul E. *Disease in the Civil War*. Springfield, IL: Charles C. Thomas, 1968.

Straubing, Harold Elk. *In Hospital and Camp: The Civil War Through the Eyes of Its Doctors and Nurses*. Harrisburg, PA: Stackpole Books, 1993.

Websites About Medicine in the Civil War

Civil War Battlefield Medicine: http://members.aol.com/cwsurgeon0/indexJ.html

Civil War Medicine: http://www.civilwarhome.com/civilwarmedicineintro.htm

Civil War and 19th Century Medical Terminology: http://members.aol.com/jweaver300/grayson/medterm.

National Museum of Civil War Medicine: http://www.civilwarmed.org

Index

Adams, George Worthington, 28, 52, 57
Alexander, Edward Porter, 28
Ambulance Corps Bill, 39
Amputations, 54, 55-56
Andersonville, 49
Anesthesia, 55
Antietam, battle of, 15, 35, 41
Antiseptics, 58
Army Medical Library, 38
Army Medical Museum, 38
Association for the Relief of Maimed Soldiers, 21

Barnes, Joseph K., 37
Beauregard, Pierre G., 48
Bellows, Henry W., 31
Bowditch, Henry I., 39

Camp Sumter, 49
Carrington, William A., 22
Chancellorsville, battle of, 21
Chesnut, Mary B., 22
Chimborazo Hospital, 22-23, 24, 49, 51
Confederate army
  ambulance service in, 20-21
  casualties in, 12, 15, 24-25
  establishment of, 11, 12
  hospitals of, 22-25
  medical department of, 15, 16-18
  relief associations of, 21
  surgeons in, 19, 20, 22
Corinth, Mississippi, 48-49
Cox, Jacob D., 14
Crane, Stephen, 11
Cumming, Kate, 24, 56-57

Davis, Jefferson, 16
DeLeon, David C., 16
Diarrhea, 46, 47, 49
Diseases, 45-52
Dix, Dorothea, 29-30
Dysentery, 46, 47, 48, 49-50

5th Colorado Artillery Regiment, 46
1st Minnesota Regiment, 15
1st Texas Regiment, 15
Fredericksburg, battle of, 14, 28, 36

Gangrene, 57
General Order Number 45, 20
General Order Number 51, 48
General Order Number 60, 20
General Order Number 100, 20
General Order Number 147, 34
Georgia Relief and Hospital Association, 21
Gettysburg, battle of, 14, 15, 37
Glatthaar, Joseph T., 40
Grant, Ulysses S., 24, 36, 38, 48, 49

Halleck, Henry, 39
Hammond, William Alexander, 30, 31, 32, 37, 38, 39
Harewood Hospital, 41
Hemorrhage, 55
Hospitals, field, 17, 40
Hospitals, general, 17, 22-25, 40, 41-42

Infirmary Corps, 19

Jackson, Stonewall, 20

Ladies' Soldiers' Aid Society, 21
Ladies' Soldiers' Relief Society, 21
Lane, Alexander G., 23
Laudable pus, 53, 57
Lee, Robert E., 20, 23
Letterman, Jonathan, 34, 35, 36, 38, 39
Longstreet, James, 28

Malaria, 47, 48, 50
McCaw, James Brown, 23
McClellan, George B., 20, 23, 32, 34, 39, 40
Meade, George Gordon, 38
Measles, 47, 48
Medical departments
  Confederate, 15, 16-18
  Union, 27-32, 35-36
Minié, Claude E., 13
Minié ball, 13, 54
Moore, Samuel Preston, 16-17, 18, 22

Nurses, 24, 29

Olmstead, Frederick Law, 31

Pneumonia, 47, 52
Pyemia, 57

Red Badge of Courage, The, 11
Reserve Surgical Corps, 25
Richmond Ambulance Committee, 20-21
Rifled musket, 13, 14, 54

2nd Tennessee Infantry, 46
Seven Days, battle of, 23, 32, 33

INDEX

Shiloh, battle of, 49
6th Michigan Infantry, 46
65th United States Colored
  Troops Regiment, 46
Smallpox, 47, 52
Smith, Charles H., 16
Smoothbore musket, 13
Spotsylvania, battle of, 38
Stanton, Edwin, 39
Steiner, Paul, 45
Stewards, 18
Stout, Samuel Hollingsworth, 25
Strong, Robert Hale, 53, 55, 59

32nd Missouri Infantry, 46
Tripler, Charles S., 32, 33, 34,
  39, 40, 47, 48
Tuberculosis, 47

26th North Carolina Infantry, 15
Typhoid fever, 47, 48, 51-52

Union army
  ambulance corps in, 32, 34-35,
    39
  blacks in, 40-41, 45
  casualties in 15, 28
  disease in, 32, 45-52
  hospitals of, 33, 40, 41-42
  medical department of, 27-32,
    35-36
  relief societies of, 30-31
  surgeons in, 32, 42-43
United States Colored Troops,
  40
United States Sanitary
  Commission, 31, 33-34, 39

University of Virginia, 18

Vicksburg, siege of, 36

Western Sanitary Commission,
  31
Wilderness, battle of, 24, 38, 41
Winder General Hospital, 23, 24
Women's Central Association
  of Relief, 31

Yellow Fever, 50-51

PHOTO CREDITS
Harper's Weekly: pp. 19, 35, 41, 46, 47, 50, 56, 58; Library of Congress: pp. 19, 35, 41, 46, 47, 50, 56, 58;
National Library of Medicine: pp. 10, 17, 20, 23, 24, 26, 29, 34, 36, 37, 39, 51, 59